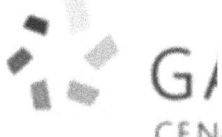

Poetry for Students, Volume 1

Staff

Marie Rose Napierkowski and Mary K. Ruby, *Editors*

David J. Kelly, Paul Mooney, Alan R. Velie, *Contributing Writers*

Gerald Barterian, Suzanne Dewsbury, David Galens, Jennifer Gariepy, Marie Lazzari, Tom Ligotti, Anna J. Sheets, Lynn M. Spampinato, Diane Telgen, Lawrence J. Trudeau, Kathleen Wilson, *Contributing Editors*

Michael L. LaBlanc, *Managing Editor*

Jeffery Chapman, *Programmer/Analyst*

Victoria B. Cariappa, *Research Team Manager*
Michele P. LaMeau, Andy Guy Malonis, Barb McNeil, Gary Oudersluys, Maureen Richards, *Research Specialists*
Julia C. Daniel, Tamara C. Nott, Tracie A.

Richardson, Cheryl L. Warnock, *Research Associates*

Susan M. Trosky, *Permissions Manager*
Kimberly F. Smilay, *Permissions Specialist*
Sarah Chesney, *Permissions Associate*
Steve Cusack, Kelly A. Quin, *Permissions Assistants*

Mary Beth Trimper, *Production Director*
Evi Seoud, *Assistant Production Manager*
Shanna Heilveil, *Production Assistant*

Randy Bassett, *Image Database Supervisor*
Mikal Ansari, Robert Duncan, *Imaging Specialists*
Pamela A. Reed, *Photography Coordinator*

Cynthia Baldwin, *Product Design Manager*
Cover design: Michelle DiMercurio, *Art Director*
Page design: Pamela A. E. Galbreath, *Senior Art Director*

Since this page cannot legibly accommodate all copyright notices, the acknowledgments constitute an extension of the copyright notice.

While every effort has been made to secure permission to reprint material and to ensure the reliability of the information presented in this publication, Gale Research neither guarantees the accuracy of the data contained herein nor assumes any responsibility for errors, omissions, or discrepancies. Gale accepts no payment for listing; and inclusion in the publication of any organization, agency, institution, publication, service, or individual does not imply endorsement of the editors or publisher. Errors brought to the attention of the publisher and verified to the satisfaction of the publisher will be corrected in future editions.

This publication is a creative work fully protected by all applicable copyright laws, as well as by misappropriation, trade secret, unfair competition, and other applicable laws. The authors and editors of this work have added value to the underlying factual material herein through one or more of the following: unique and original selection, coordination, expression, arrangement, and classification of the information.

All rights to this publication will be vigorously defended.

Copyright © 1998
Gale Research
835 Penobscot Building
645 Griswold St.
Detroit, MI 48226-4094

All rights reserved including the right of reproduction in whole or in part in any form.

This book is printed on acid-free paper that meets the minimum requirements of American National Standard for Information Sciences—Permanence Paper for Printed Library Materials, ANSI Z39.48-1984.

ISBN 0-7876-1688-5
ISSN 1094-7019

Printed in the United States of America
10 9 8 7

My Last Duchess

Robert Browning 1842

Introduction

First published in the collection *Dramatic Lyrics* in 1842, "My Last Duchess" is an excellent example of Browning's use of dramatic monologue. Browning's psychological portrait of a powerful Renaissance aristocrat is presented to the reader as if he or she were simply "eavesdropping" on a slice of casual conversation. As the poem unfolds, the reader learns the speaker of the poem, Duke Ferrara, is talking to a representative of his fiancee's family. Standing in front of a portrait of the Duke's last wife, now dead, the Duke talks about the woman's failings and imperfections. The irony of the poem surfaces as the reader discovers that the young woman's "faults" were qualities like compassion, modesty, humility, delight in simple pleasures, and courtesy to those who served her.

Using abundant detail, Browning leads the reader to conclude that the Duke found fault with his former wife because she did not reserve her attentions for him, his rank, and his power. More importantly, the Duke's long list of complaints presents a thinly veiled threat about the behavior he will and will not tolerate in his new wife. The lines "I gave commands; / smiles stopped together" suggest that the Duke somehow, directly or indirectly, brought about the death of the last Duchess. In this dramatic monologue, Browning has not only depicted the inner workings of his speaker, but has in fact allowed the speaker to reveal his own failings and imperfections to the reader.

Author Biography

Browning was born in 1812 in Camberwell, a suburb of London, to middle-class parents. His father Robert Browning, Sr., a clerk for the Bank of England, possessed cultivated artistic and literary tastes; his mother, Sarah Anne Wiedemann, was a devout Christian who pursued interests in music and nature. Browning was an intellectually precocious child who read at the age of five and composed his first poetry at six. He read widely from his father's extensive rare book collection, acquiring an abundant, if unsystematic, knowledge of a broad range of different literatures. At ten Browning began Peckam School, where he remained for four years. In 1828 he entered London University but quit school after less than a year, determined to pursue a career as a poet. Browning lived with his parents until 1846 and so was able to devote his entire energies to his art.

His literary career began in 1833 with the anonymous publication of the long poem *Pauline: A Fragment of a Confession*. This was followed by *Paracelsus* (1835) and *Sordello* (1840). All three of these early works met with mostly negative reviews. Beginning in 1841 Browning published a series of eight pamphlets collectively titled *Bells and Pomegranates* (1841-45). The series contains narrative poems, including *Pippa Passes* (1841); verse dramas; and two collections of shorter pieces, *Dramatic Lyrics* (1842) and *Dramatic Romances and Lyrics* (1845). Although Browning had to this point failed to win either popular or critical esteem, his work did gain the admiration of Elizabeth Barrett, who was a respected and popular poet in her own right. In 1844 she praised Browning in one of her works and received a grateful letter from him in response. They met the following year, fell in love, and in 1846, ignoring the disapproval of her father, eloped to Italy, where they spent the remainder of their life together. Their son Robert Wiedemann Barrett Browning was born in 1849.

In Italy Browning continued to write, and though public success still eluded him, his works attracted increasing respect from critics. Following Elizabeth's death in 1861, he and his son returned to England. The appearance in 1864 of the collection *Dramatis Personae* finally brought Browning his first significant critical and popular acclaim. In 1868-69 he published *The Ring and the Book,* a series of dramatic monologues in which various speakers relate different perspectives on an actual seventeenth-century Italian murder case. Tremendously popular, *The Ring and the Book* firmly established Browning's reputation. From 1868 on, Browning was generally regarded as one of England's greatest living poets. He remained highly productive, and the publication of his *Dramatic Idyls* (1879-80) and other works brought him worldwide fame. In 1881 the Browning Society was established in London for the purpose of studying his poems. Near the end of his life he was the recipient of various honors, including a degree from Oxford University and an audience with

Queen Victoria. Following his death in 1889 during a stay in Venice, he was buried in Poet's Corner of Westminster Abbey.

Poem Text

Ferrara

That's my last Duchess painted on the wall,
Looking as if she were alive. I call
That piece a wonder, now: Frà Pandolf's hands
Worked busily a day, and there she stands.
Will't please you sit and look at her? I said
"Frà Pandolf" by design, for never read
Strangers like you that pictured countenance,
The depth and passion of its earnest glance,
But to myself they turned (since none puts by
The curtain I have drawn for you, but I)
And seemed as they would ask me, if they durst,
How such a glance came there; so, not the first
Are you to turn and ask thus. Sir, 'twas not
Her husband's presence only, called

that spot
Of joy into the Duchess' cheek; perhaps
Frà Pandolf chanced to say, "Her mantle laps
Over my lady's wrist too much," or "Paint
Must never hope to reproduce the faint
Half-flush that dies along her throat": such stuff
Was courtesy, she thought, and cause enough
For calling up that spot of joy. She had
A heart—how shall I say?—too soon made glad,
Too easily impressed: she liked whate'er
She looked on, and her looks went everywhere.
Sir, 'twas all one! My favour at her breast,
The dropping of the daylight in the West,
The bough of cherries some officious fool
Broke in the orchard for her, the white mule
She rode with round the terrace—all and each
Would draw from her alike the approving speech,

Or blush, at least. She thanked men,
—good! but thanked
Somehow—I know not how—as if she ranked
My gift of a nine-hundred-years-old name
With anybody's gift. Who'd stoop to blame
This sort of trifling? Even had you skill
In speech—(which I have not)—to make your will
Quite clear to such an one, and say, "Just this
Or that in you disgusts me; here you miss,
Or there exceed the mark"—and if she let
Herself be lessoned so, nor plainly set
Her wits to yours, forsooth, and made excuse,
—E'en then would be some stooping; and I choose
Never to stoop. Oh sir, she smiled, no doubt,
Whene'er I passed her; but who passed without
Much the same smile? This grew; I gave commands;
Then all smiles stopped together. There she stands
As if alive. Will't please you rise?

We'll meet
The company below, then. I repeat,
The Count your master's known munificence
Is ample warrant that no just pretence
Of mine for dowry will be disallowed;
Though his fair daughter's self, as I avowed
At starting, is my object. Nay, we'll go
Together down, sir. Notice Neptune, though,
Taming a sea-horse, thought a rarity,
Which Claus of Innsbruck cast in bronze for me!

Poem Summary

Lines 1-2

The beginning note is meant to explain to that the speaker of the poem is the Duke of Ferrara; this provides the reader with location (Italy) and class environment (aristocratic). In the opening lines Browning sets the scene for the poem, focusing the reader's imagination on the painting on the wall. The central premise of the poem is put in place: the dead wife will appear to come back to life only through the artistry of the picture. Through this, Browning allows the reader to begin to think of the woman as a real person, once very much alive, and initiates a "relationship" between the dead woman and the reader. Once the reader begins to feel sympathy for the woman, then the subsequent "reasons" given by the Duke concerning her "imperfections" will seem all the more outrageous.

Lines 3-4

Here, Browning accomplishes two things: a) an emphasis on the mastery of the artist, "Frà Pandolf," who created a work of art that makes the dead woman seem so animated; and b) an introduction to the Duke's subtle, mocking tone with the phrases "piece of wonder" and "busily a day". These words seem to be heavy with ridicule and scorn for both woman and artist. At this point the reader might begin to think the Duke was jealous of the man who "fussed" over his wife but who, ultimately created —not a masterpiece—but just a portion of one. It should be noted that, unlike some other figures in Browning's work, Frà Pandolf—and later, Claus of Innsbruck—is an imaginary, not historical, figure.

Line 5

The use of the word "you" informs the reader that there is an immediate addressee within the fiction of the poem; the speaker is not addressing the reader, but another character. More specifically, it indicates that the speaker of the poem, the Duke, is now addressing the emissary directly, asking him to sit and gaze upon picture of the dead woman. The reader may imagine the emissary sitting in a chair while the Duke stands and delivers his speech. In effect, the emissary is now in a subordinate position.

Lines 6-9

The words "by design" imply that the artist is well-known and has some prestige attached to his name. The Duke may want to advertise that it was his own talent for hiring the right artist that was responsible for the "lifelike quality" of the picture. The Duke also stresses that all of the painting's viewers—"strangers like you"—remark upon the painting's lifelike look. In addition, the Duke appears more taken with the painting than with the real woman the picture represents. The image of emotion—the "passion" in the "glance"—seems more valuable to him than genuine emotion. The use of the word "its" instead of "her" suggests that the Duke has more of a relationship with the painting than he did with his dead wife. With these details, Browning begins to interject the notion of the Duke's jealousy. That "passionate glance" might have been placed there by the painter, whom the Duke probably sees as a rival for his dead wife's affection.

Lines 10-13

These lines suggest just how striking the depth and passion of the image are, since apparently all previous viewers have wanted to know what excited the Duchess enough to inspire that look in her eyes. The Duke also betrays his possessiveness and desire for control when he comments that "none puts by / The curtain ... but I."

Lines 14-15

At this point, Browning suggests more of the Duke's possessiveness, as he tells the emissary that it wasn't his presence alone that made his wife happy or caused the "spot of joy," which may literally have been a blush. The Duke insinuates that this blush must have come to her face from either being in the company of a lover or from her far too impressionable and undiscriminating nature.

Lines 16-21

The Duke begins to offer his guesses at what, aside from some illicit pleasure, might have caused the Duchess to blush. Two readings are possible, turning on the reader's sense of how seriously the Duke believes in the monk's vows of celibacy. If the painter was not the Duchess' lover, then her nature was simply too susceptible to flattery for the Duke's liking.

Lines 22-34

This section of the poem begins the Duke's long list of complaints against the Duchess. First and foremost, she was innocent, too easily pleased and impressed. He blames her for not seeing any difference between being the wife of a "great man" and: being able to see the sunset; receiving a bouquet from someone of status below the Duke's; or riding a white mule. While he thinks it's fine to be courteous ("She thanked men,—good!"), she gave all men the kind of respect that only a man with his family's rank and distinction deserves.

Lines 35-43

Having recounted the Duchess's imperfections, the Duke announces that, even though her faults were many, he would not lower himself—"stoop"—by telling her what bothered him. Note how the Duke tries to paint himself as a "plain-spoken" man, one who has no "skill" in "speech." At this point in the poem, the reader may realize the Duke is well-skilled in the uses of language. The Duke explains that, even if he had the skill to tell the Duchess just how much she disgusted him, he would not have explained to her how and why her actions bothered him. On one hand, he betrays a fear that she would have argued with him: "plainly set / Her wits to yours." On the other hand, he explains that the very process of having to explain his feelings to her would have constituted a compromise (or "stoop") to his authority.

Lines 44-48

These lines contain the speaker's final judgement on the Duchess. The Duke recalls his dead wife's smile, and how she never reserved her smile for him. The lines "gave commands; / Then all smiles stopped together" tell us that the Duke used his power to curb his wife's friendliness, but the words also leave the details ambiguous. At best, he may have restricted her behavior in a way that dampened her ardor for life; at worst, he may have ordered her assassination. The next lines, with the emphasis on "as if alive," underscore her death.

Lines 49-53

As the poem draws to a close, the Duke redirects his attention to his upcoming marriage. He tells the emissary that he is certain his future bride's father will give him a generous dowry. The Duke, however, wants to be seen as a man who is more interested in his fiancee than in any money she might bring to their union. At this point, the reader is unlikely to trust these declarations and is likely to fear for this young woman's welfare.

Lines 54-56

The poem concludes with the final image of a god, "Neptune ," taming a seahorse. The image of the powerful god taking control over a creature like a seahorse demonstrates the relationship between the Duke (Neptune) and the last Duchess (seahorse). It is as if, by pointing out this sculpture to the emissary, the Duke is restating his power over his future bride, as well as his more general power in the world. The final lines emphasize another aspect of that power, showing not just the Duke's desire to possess rare objects of beauty, but also his ability to do so.

Themes

Pride

The speaker's overbearing pride—or in moral terms, his hubris—is incorporated into the very situation of Browning's monologue. In it, the Duke addresses an inferior, the emissary of a nobleman ("the Count, your master") whose daughter he intends to make his second wife. There are financial negotiations at stake—the matter of a dowry that the Duke intends to collect from the Count. In fact, the Duke seems in the process of acquiring in the next Duchess an "object," to use his own word. But the actual amount of money is not the real issue. The Duke suggests that among noblemen, whose behaviors are governed by "just pretense," no reasonable monetary request would be denied; the negotiations, then, are in one sense a mere formality. In a second sense, however, money functions symbolically, both in the Duke's mind and for the reader trying to understand the Duke's motives. In his world, after all, people can be bought and sold, and the terms of their existence can determined by those like the Duke who possess all the power in a hierarchical society. Thus, the negotiations are really about the conditions under which the Count's daughter will become the Duke's wife—conditions that amount to, the Duke suggests, absolute submission to his pride.

Topics for Further Study

- Much has been said about the Duke's account of his former wife's fate: "I gave commands; / Then all smiles stopped together." What precisely does the Duke mean by these lines? How can we tell? Why do you think Browning lets the Duke express the most dramatic part of his story in such brief and cryptic terms?

- The Duke reproaches the late Duchess' character, but the reader might come away from the poem with an entirely different view of her. What can we tell about the Duchess from the Duke's own account of her? What does his description of her "shortcomings" tell us about her, and what do they tell us about the Duke?

- Part of the poem's impact comes from the Duke's certainty that he has behaved properly. As an exercise, write a two-page monologue in which someone confesses to a crime for which he feels no remorse. Before you begin, consider your approach. What tone will your speaker adopt? What words will he choose to describe the crime itself? What justification can he offer for what he has done?

To stress this point, the Duke describes the fate of his former wife, his "last duchess." It is here that we see the juxtaposition of the Duke's corrupt pride and the Duchess' pureness. Though he describes her affronts to his arrogant nature, she comes across as a warm and lively woman, one loved by everybody for her ability to enjoy life. Yet her pleasant demeanor evoked jealousy in the Duke: she was "too soon made glad, / too easily impressed: she liked whate'er / she looked on, and her looks went everywhere." He found it insulting that she equated his "gift of a nine-hundred-years-old name" with "anybody's gift." Clinging to his pride, however, he considered it a form of "trifling" to display his resentment or to discuss his feelings with the Duchess—it would have amounted to "stooping," and the Duke "chose never to stoop." Instead, he "gave commands," and the Duchess' "looks stopped altogether." Thus, the Duke felt it was better to dispense with the Duchess altogether than to live with a woman whose devotion was not—he believed—focused entirely upon him.

Art and Experience

The Duke's monologue both begins and concludes with the Duke drawing his listener's attention to works of art: first, the painting of the "last Duchess," his former wife; in the final lines, a sculpture of the sea-god Neptune taming a "seahorse." Because of this, the entire monologue—ostensibly about the failings of the late Duchess—is actually couched in the aesthetic terms the Duke applies to human relationships. But precisely what are those terms? On one level, they seem wrapped in the same corrupt arrogance that led to the demise of his first wife. As he exhibits the painting and sculpture, it is clear he wants the listener to admire not so much the works themselves as him. If they are beautiful, such beauty exists as proof of the Duke's excellent taste and his connections with the best artists of his day. His aesthetic sense, then, is equal to his ambition: he is obsessed with the ownership and control of beauty itself. This is evident in the way he describes the shortcomings of the former Duchess, who was beautiful but refused to be "owned" in such a way, and in his commentary on the Neptune sculpture, which he admires less for its intrinsic value than for the fact it is "thought a rarity" and has been cast by a famous artist "for me."

On a second level, it becomes clear the Duke's refined taste as a collector bears no relation to the humanistic qualities of the art itself. In the sculpture, he misses the irony we perceive: that Neptune, "taming" a creature of natural beauty and freedom, is in fact symbolic of the Duke himself. He also fails to understand that his appreciation for the skill with which the Duchess has been rendered on canvas is incongruous with his lack of appreciation for the painting's real-life subject. In this way, he has not only assigned art a higher place than life—he has also credited to art the qualities it draws from life. Thus, he is able to replace a living wife with a portrait of one: "That's my last Duchess painted on the wall," he says, "looking as if she were alive." While he reproaches the woman herself, he deems the painting "a wonder"—a form of perfection that, in his opinion at least, life itself cannot approach.

Style

"My Last Duchess" is written in rhymed iambic pentameter, which maintains an even beat throughout the poem.

Iambic pentameter has been said to be the most natural cadence of the English language. It consists of an iamb, which is two syllables: an unstressed followed by a stressed. An example of an iamb might be the words "a heart," drawn from the lines: "A heart—how shall I say? too soon made glad." The rhythm of the first two words can be scanned with emphasis indicating a stressed syllable, and an unstressed syllable:

> a **heart**.

Pentameter means that there are five groups of iambs in a line of poetry; each group is called a foot.

"My Last Duchess" also uses rhymed couplets, meaning that every two lines end with a rhyme. For example, the first two lines of the poem end with the words "wall" and "call." The poetic device of the rhymed couplet, however, is balanced by the use of enjambment, which creates the more natural cadence of a conversation. This technique also helps to keep the even rhythm of iambic pentameter from sounding too monotonous. The poem interrupts itself—much as the speaker of the poem interrupts himself—by inserting a question here ("how shall I say?") or a parenthetical comment there "(since none puts by / The curtain I have drawn for you, but I)". This device also helps to illustrate how the Duke's true motivations are breaking through the surface of his everyday language.

Historical Context

Browning's poem, which is set in Renaissance Italy, may tell us less about the Renaissance itself than about Victorian views toward the period. The incident the poem dramatizes comes from the life of Alfonso II, a nobleman of Spanish origin who was Duke of Ferrara in Italy during the sixteenth century. Alfonso's first wife was Lucrezia, a member of the Italian Borgia family and the daughter of a man who later became pope. Although she died only three years into the marriage—to be replaced, as the poem suggests, by the daughter of the Count of Tyrol—Lucrezia transformed the court of Ferrara into a gathering place for Renaissance artists, including the famous Venetian painter Titian. As a result, Ferrara became exemplary of the aesthetic awakening that was taking place throughout Italy.

The term Renaissance, from the French word, actually means "rebirth," and the time to which it refers is characterized by cultural and intellectual developments as much as by political events. During the Renaissance, which is generally defined as the period 1350 to 1700, Europeans experienced the resurrection of classical Greek and Roman ideals that had remained dormant since the collapse of the Roman Empire in the fifth century. Artists and thinkers of the Renaissance believed that classical art, science, philosophy, and literature had been lost during the "dark ages" that followed the fall of Rome. They held that these ideals waited to be rediscovered, and Italians in particular believed themselves to be the true heirs to Roman achievement. For this reason, it was natural that the Renaissance should begin in Italy, where the ruins of ancient civilization provided a continual reminder of the classical past and where other artistic movements—the Gothic, for instance—had never taken firm hold.

Especially in Italy, the artistic achievement of the Renaissance was facilitated by a system of patronage: wealthy individuals commissioned paintings, sculptures, and buildings to glorify their own achievements. The works of such artists as Michelangelo, Leonardo da Vinci, Raphael, and Donatello come to us as a direct result of such patronage, and their visions reflect the ideals of the period. Foremost among Renaissance ideals was that of humanism. Like the ancient Greeks and Romans, Renaissance artists and thinkers valued the condition of earthly life, glorified man's nature, and celebrated individual achievement. These attitudes combined to form a new spirit of optimism—the belief that man was capable of accomplishing great things.

Compare & Contrast

- **1842:** English social reformer Edwin Chadwick publishes "Sanitary Conditions of the Labouring Population of Great Britain." The report, which exposes the poor conditions and high disease rate among England's factory workers, shocks the public and raises the need for reform.

Today: While the living conditions of workers in advanced nations remain acceptable, annual United Nations reports on conditions in Third World countries show workers experience ongoing poverty, disease, and occupational danger.

- **1843:** A British force of 2,800 men under Sir Charles Napier defeats a 30,000-man Baluch Army, forcing India's Muslim emirs of Sind to surrender their independence to the East India Company.

    Today: Great Britain relinquishes Hong Kong, the jewel of its remaining Asian colonial possessions, to the Republic of China. To many, the event symbolizes the increasing transfer of European power to other parts of the world.

- **1846:** After a series of crop failures, Parliament repeals the Corn Laws, reducing tariff duties on imported goods and opening the door to free trade.

Today: Britain's political debate centers on whether the country should relinquish the pound in favor of the Euro. The single multinational currency is favored by the European Union, which proposes to make Europe a single economic entity.

But there was a dark side to the Renaissance, and people of Browning's era often took a dim view toward the era as a whole. In some ways, this view was a subtle acknowledgment of the Victorians' own shortcomings and fears. For instance, just as Renaissance humanism seemed to elevate man at the expense of God, the Victorians found themselves puzzling over God's existence in light of Darwinism. Similarly, the Victorians' own experience demonstrated that the high points of civilization and progress do not necessarily coincide with moral virtues. As England was fighting colonial wars and grappling with mass poverty in its factory towns, Victorians looked at the Renaissance for a sense of moral superiority. And they had certain justification to do so. For all its cultural achievement, the Renaissance was rife with corruption, perversity, and violence. The same power that allowed wealthy families to commission great art also enabled them to crush rival individuals or even cities, and nearly all the noble art patrons—including the Borgia family, of whom the historical "last Duchess" was a member—had murders to answer for.

Critical Overview

In general, critics have agreed on many basic interpretive issues about "My Last Duchess." William DeVane appears to voice common opinion when he characterizes the last Duchess as an obvious victim—as "outraged innocence" trapped in an age when "no god came to the rescue." Readers also easily agree that the dramatic monologue works ironically, presenting a meaning at odds with the speaker's intention: that is, the more the Duke says, the more he loses the reader's sympathy. Critics also concur that "My Last Duchess" exemplifies two important elements of Browning's talent for dramatic monologue: his ability to evoke the unconstrained reaction of a person in a particular situation or crisis and his use of history to provide the appropriate historical context.

In support of the first element, William O. Raymond, writing for *Studies in Philology* suggests that "My Last Duchess" is a "masterpiece" because it "fuses character and incident, thought and emotion." Raymond, as other critics have also argued, suggests that the poet uses dramatic monologue to create or isolate a single moment in which the character reveals himself most starkly. In 1982 Clyde de L. Ryals extended this assertion a little further, arguing that the Duke not only "tells all" in this unguarded moment, but further that he "attempts to justify it," revealing even more of himself in the process.

Many readers have also noted that the poet creates an important historical context for the Duke, and the values he reveals, by setting the poem in Renaissance Italy. Values that might strike us today and may even have struck Browning's nineteenth-century readers as unacceptable—possessiveness, haughtiness, love of power—could have been expected in a Renaissance aristocrat, thus accounting for at least some of the Duke's self-importance. Along these lines, several critics have praised the poem for its historical accuracy. Robert Langbaum, in his 1957 book *The Poetry of Experience; The Dramatic Monologue in Modern Literary Tradition,* contends that "we accept the combination of villainy with taste and manners as a phenomenon of the Renaissance and of the old aristocratic order generally."

Langbaum introduces a less evident point when he asserts that Browning's poem takes the reader beyond acceptance to actual sympathy with or admiration for the Duke. Langbaum acknowledges that the Duchess is the first object of reader sympathy—"no summary or paraphrase would indicate that condemnation is not our principle response"—but also proposes that the form of dramatic monologue disposes the reader to suspend moral judgement and possibly to identify with the Duke. Not only do we admire the Duke's power and taste, according to Langbaum, but we also have no choice but to be "overwhelmed" by his speech, just as the envoy is. Ryals echoes this reading in 1982 when he contends that, because the Duke "is a fascinating character, bigger than life," the reader must hold "two conflicting views of the same individual."

Sources

DeVane, William C., "The Virgin and the Dragon," in *The Yale Review* Vol. XXXVII, No. 1, September, 1947, pp. 33-46.

Friedland, Louis S., "Ferrara and *My Last Duchess,*" in *Studies in Philology* Vol. 33, 1936, pp. 656-84.

Jerman, B. R., "Browning's Witless Duke," and Perrine, Laurence, "Browning's Shrewd Duke," in *Publications of the Modern Language Association* Vol. 72, June, 1957, pp. 488-93.

Langbaum, Robert, *The Poetry of Experience: The Dramatic Monologue in Modern Literary Tradition* New York: Random House, 1963.

Langbaum, Robert, "The Dramatic Monologue: Sympathy versus Judgement," in *The Poetry of Experience: The Dramatic Monologue in Modern Literary Tradition,* Random House, 1957, pp. 75-108.

Raymond, William O., "Browning's Casuists," in *Studies in Philology,* Vol. XXXVII, No. 4, October, 1940, pp. 641-66.

Ryals, Clyde de L., "Browning's Irony," in *The Victorian Experience: The Poets,* edited by Richard A. Levine, Ohio University Press, 1982, pp. 23-46.

For Further Study

Atlick, Richard D., *Victorian People and Ideas,* New York: Norton, 1973.

> An overview of Victorian culture and history, presented thematically as a companion to the literature of the age.

McCarthy, Mary, *The Stones of Florence,* New York: Harvest Books, 1963.

> Writing about its most significant city, McCarthy paints a compelling picture of the Renaissance in all its glory and corruption.

Pater, Walter, *The Renaissance,* Chicago: Pandora Books, 1978.

> A Victorian, Pater resurrects the great figures of the Renaissance. His biographical sketches tell not only of the period about which he writes but also about his nineteenth-century audience, which had grown skeptical of its Renaissance legacy.

Lightning Source UK Ltd.
Milton Keynes UK
UKHW020944130319
339055UK00011B/327/P